CONTEST WINNERS FOR THREE

Piano Trios from the Alfred, Belwin, and Myklas Libraries

Foreword

Three is not always a crowd when making beautiful music at the piano! *Contest Winners for Three* is a time-tested collection of imaginative trios that can be an exciting part of any piano studio's curriculum, continuing to bring smiles to performers and audiences for years to come.

Alfred, Belwin, and Myklas have produced an extensive list of quality elementary- and intermediate-level piano trios over the years. The pieces included in this volume represent well-loved and effective trios drawn from festival and contest lists, presented in approximate order of difficulty. Divided into five graded collections, outstanding pieces are made available again by Jonathan Aaber, Dennis Alexander, Mary Elizabeth Clark, Margaret Goldston, Joyce Grill, Carrie Kraft, Sharon Lohse Kunitz, Beatrice Miller, Ruth Perdew, and Robert D. Vandall.

Contents

Alfred Music
P.O. Box 10003
Van Nuys, CA 91410-0003
alfred.com

ISBN-10: 0-7390-9931-0
ISBN-13: 978-0-7390-9931-5

Bob's Blues

Part 3

Robert D. Vandall

© 1981 by MYKLAS PRESS

Bob's Blues

Part 1

Moderato

RH 1 octave higher than written throughout

Robert D. Vandall

Part 2

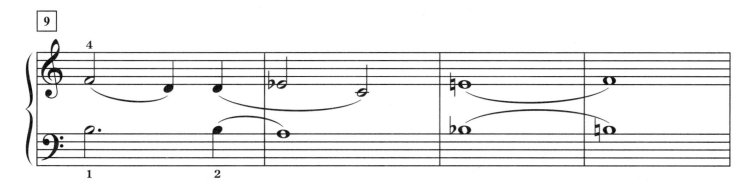

Part 3

Part 2

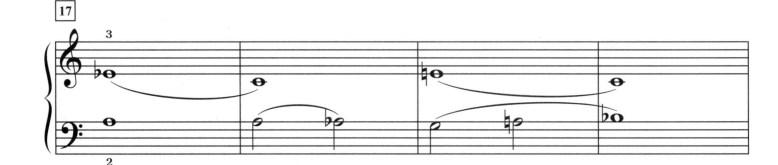

Part 1

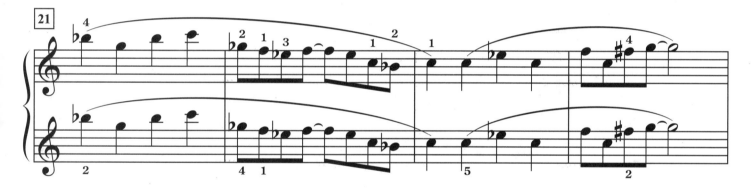

Part 2

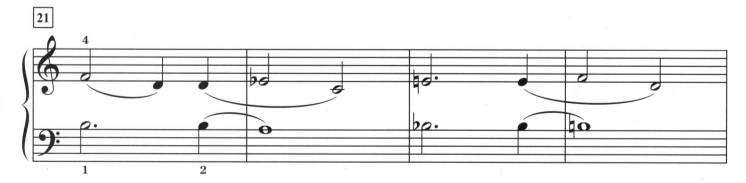

Part 3

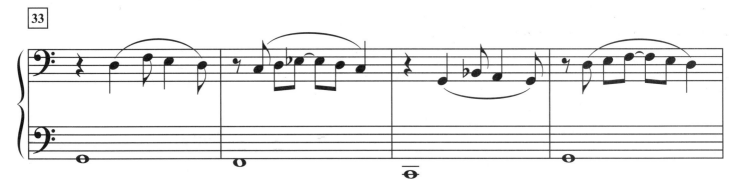

Part 2

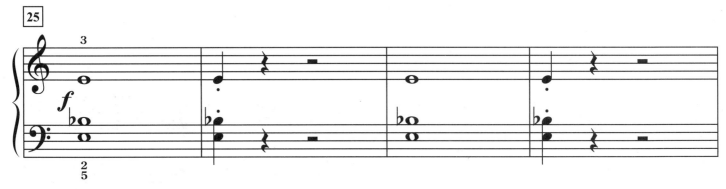

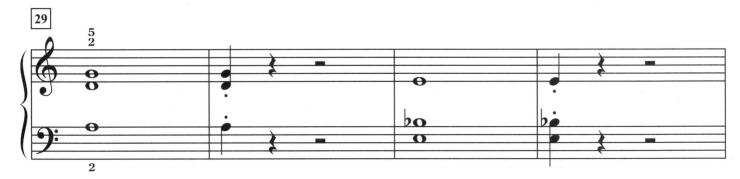

Part 1

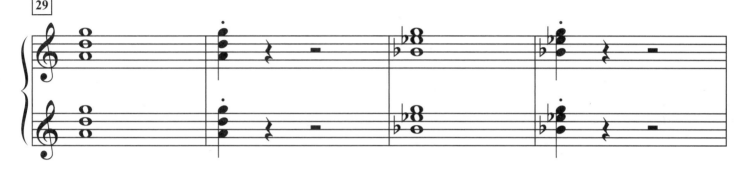

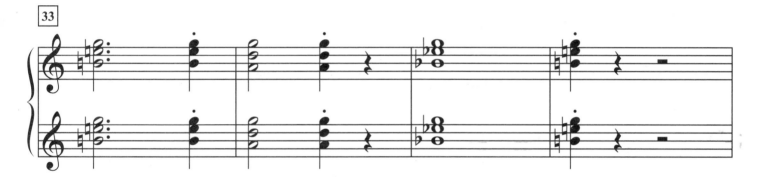

Part 2

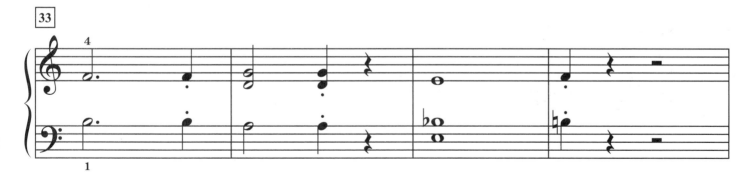

Part 3

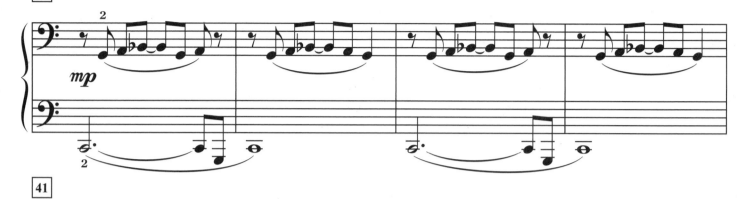

Part 2

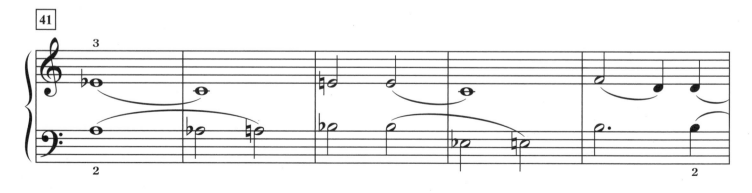

Part 1

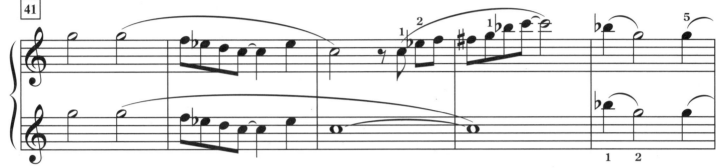

Part 2

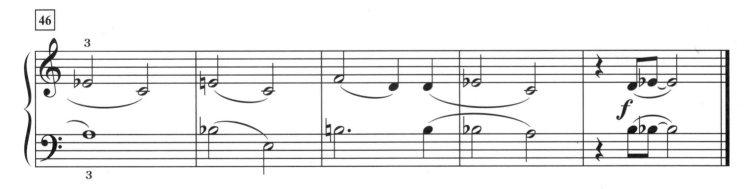

Hava Nagila

Part 3

Israeli folk song
Arr. Ruth Perdew

Part 2

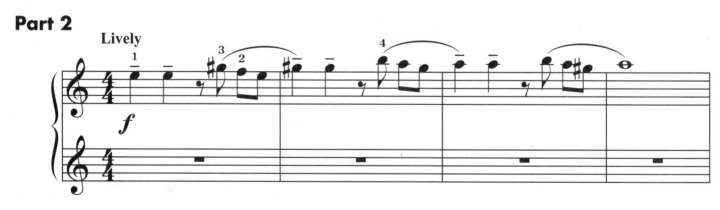

Hava Nagila

Part 1

Israeli folk song
Arr. Ruth Perdew

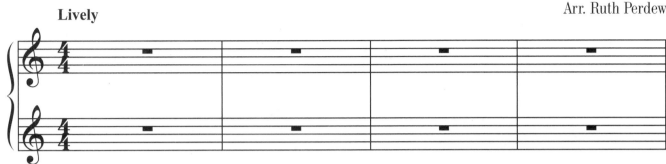

Both hands 1 octave higher than written throughout

Part 2

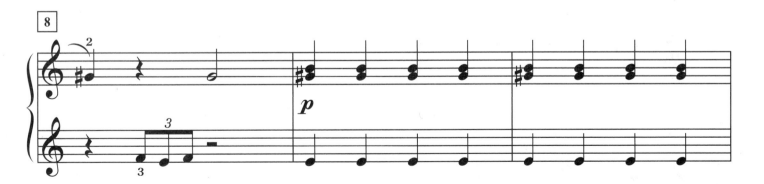

12

Part 3

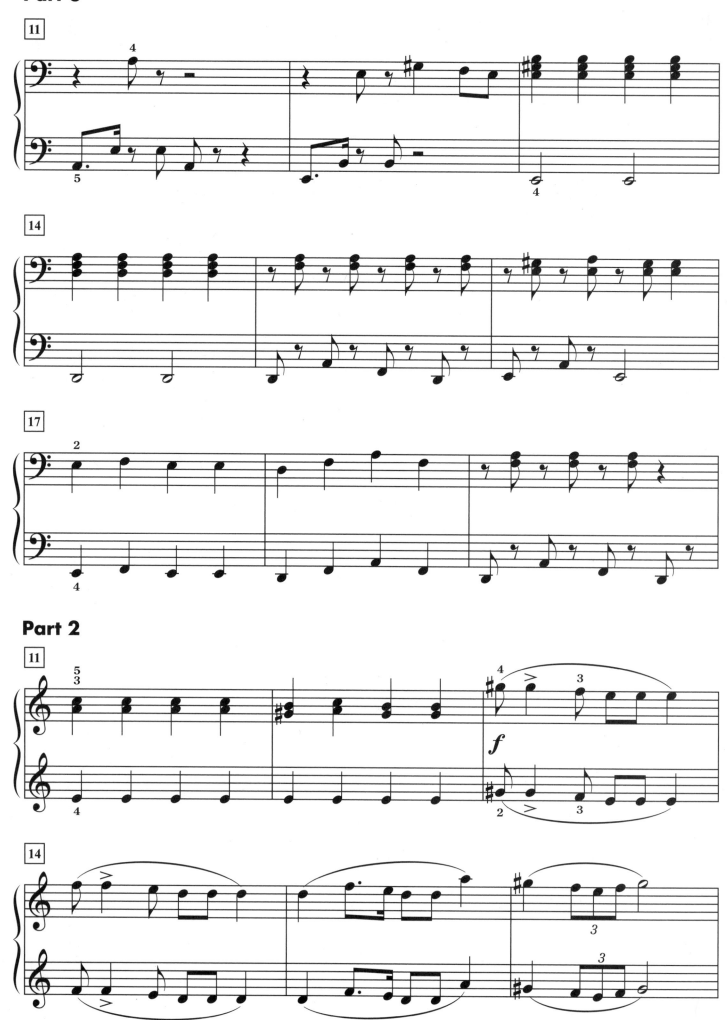

Part 2

Part 1

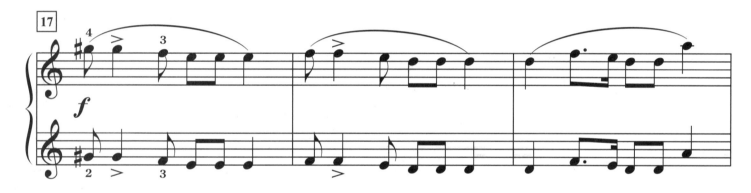

Part 2

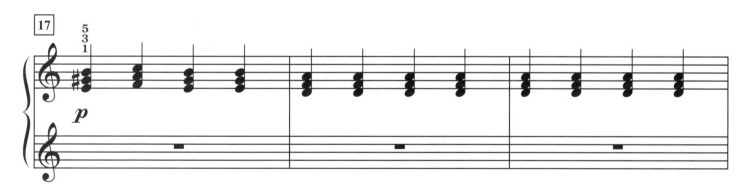

Part 3

Part 2

Part 1

Part 2

March Promenade

Part 3

Robert D. Vandall

March Promenade

Part 1

Robert D. Vandall

18

Part 3

Part 2

Part 1

Part 2

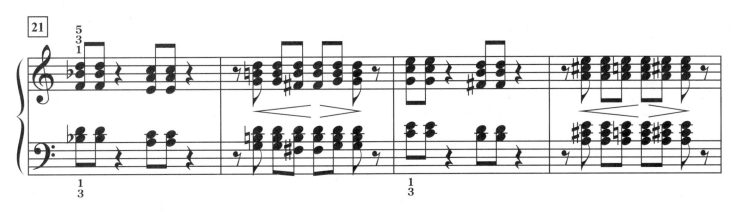

Part 3

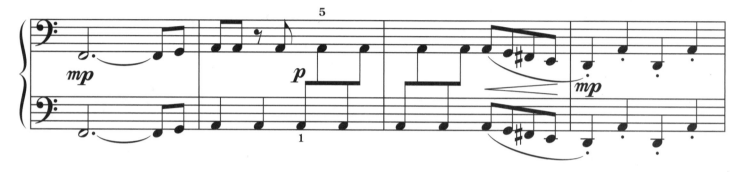

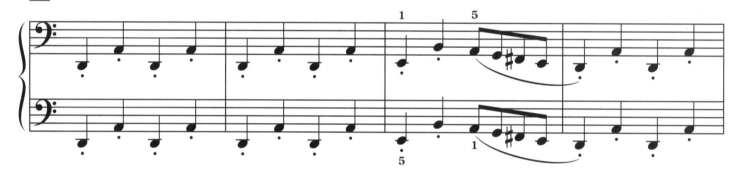

Part 2

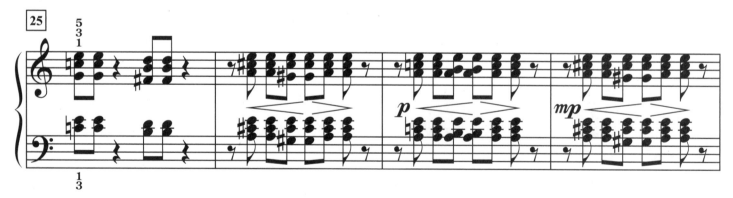

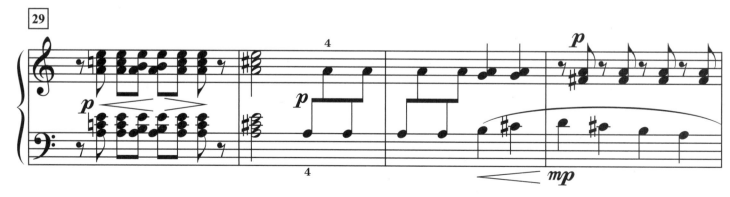

Part 1

Part 2

Part 3

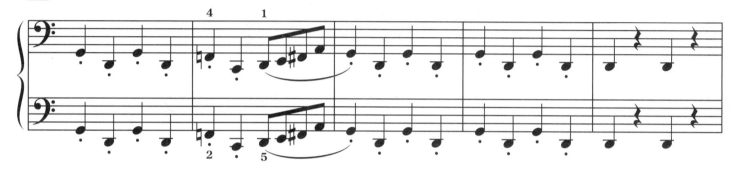

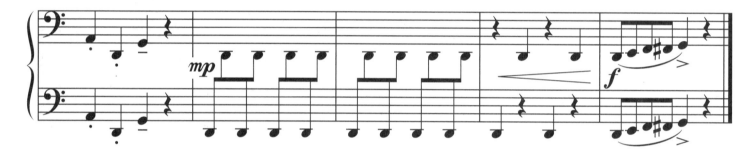

Part 2

Part 1

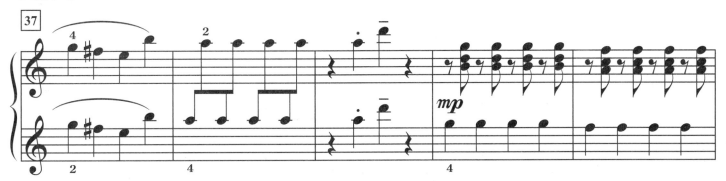

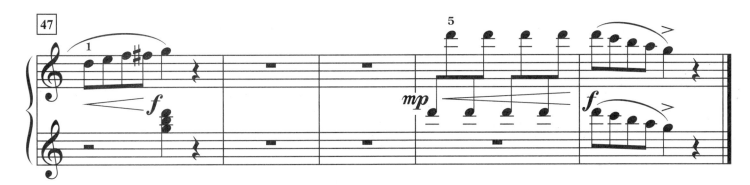

Part 2

America the Beautiful

Music by Samuel A. Ward
Words by Katharine Lee Bates
Arr. Jonathan Aaber

Part 3

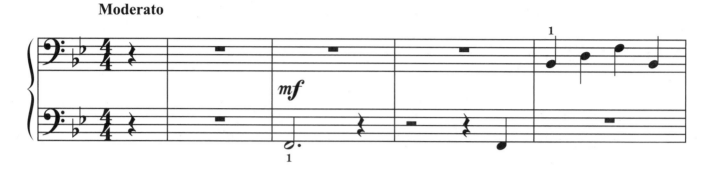

Part 2

America the Beautiful

Music by Samuel A. Ward
Words by Katharine Lee Bates
Arr. Jonathan Aaber

Part 1

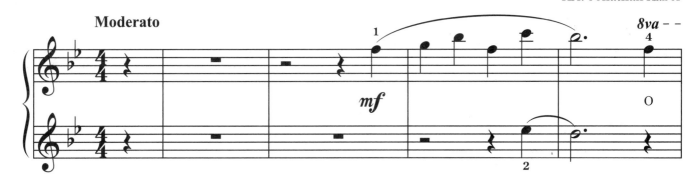

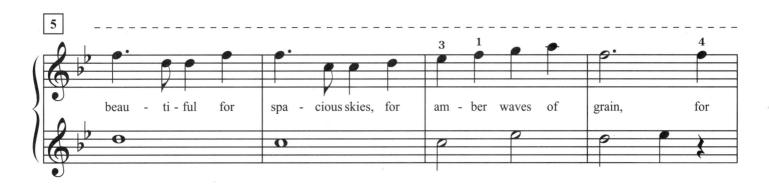

Part 2

Part 3

Part 2

Part 1

Part 2

Blue Threesome

Part 3

Robert D. Vandall

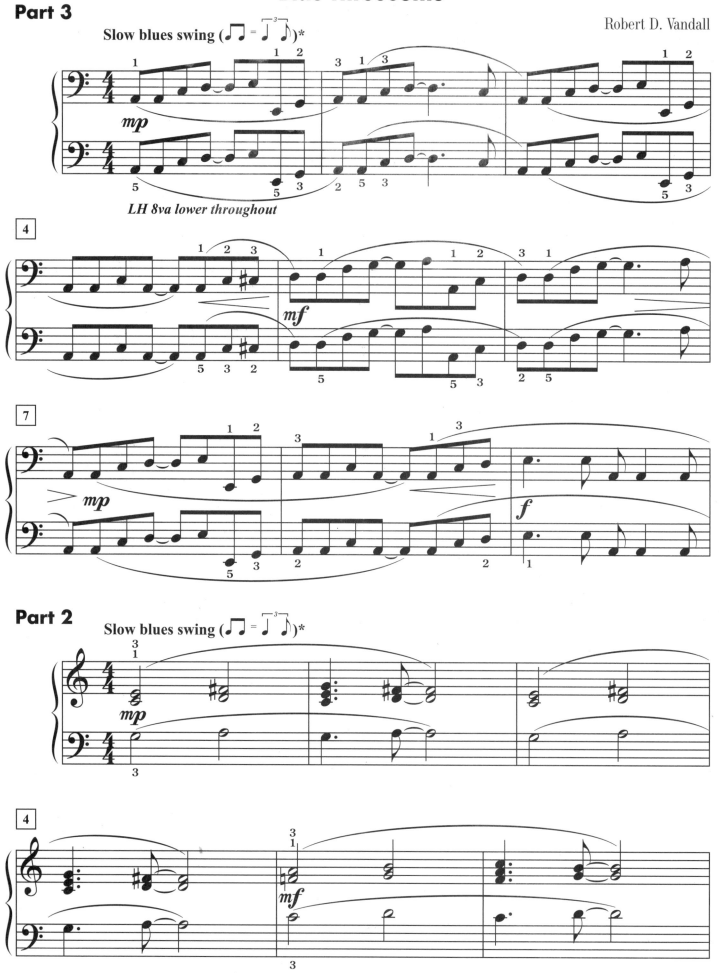

LH 8va lower throughout

Part 2

* Also effective when played with straight eighth notes.

Blue Threesome

Part 1

Robert D. Vandall

Part 2

* Also effective when played with straight eighth notes.

© 1984 BRADLEY PUBLICATIONS

Part 3

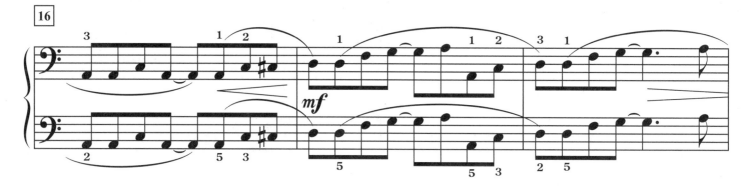

Part 2

Part 1

Part 2

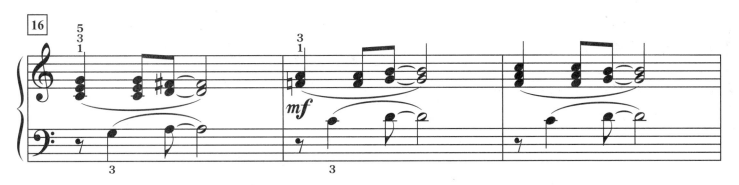

Part 3

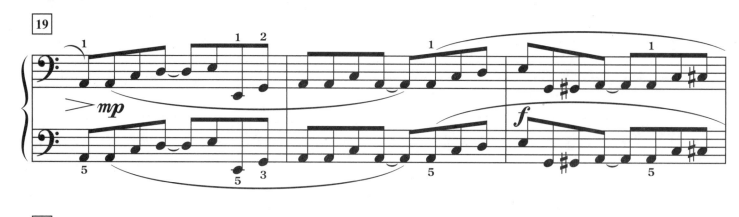

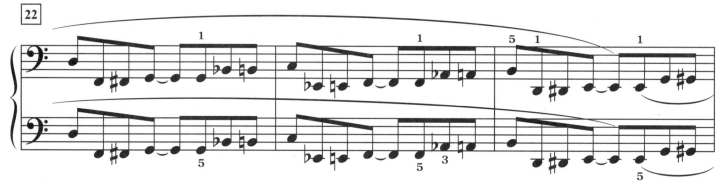

Part 2

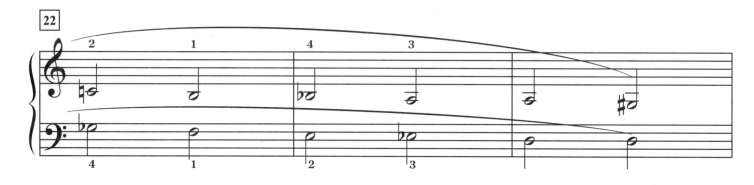

Part 1

Part 2

Polka Diana

Part 3

Ruth Perdew

Part 2

Polka Diana

Part 1

Ruth Perdew

Part 2

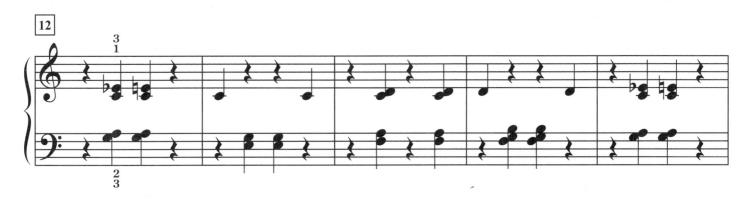

Part 3

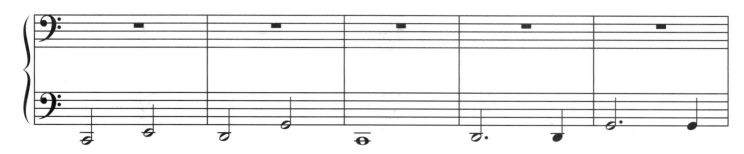

Part 2

Part 1

Part 2

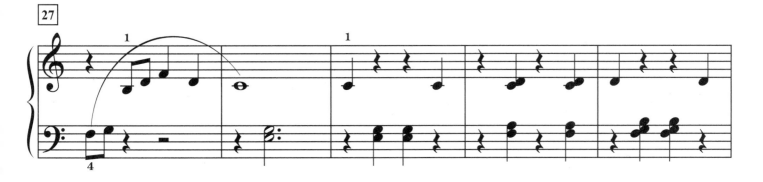

38

Part 3

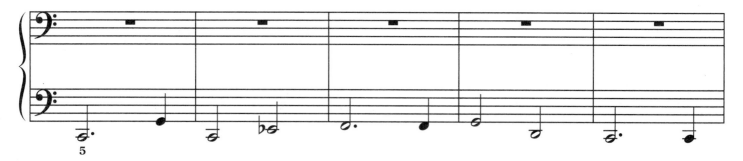

Part 2

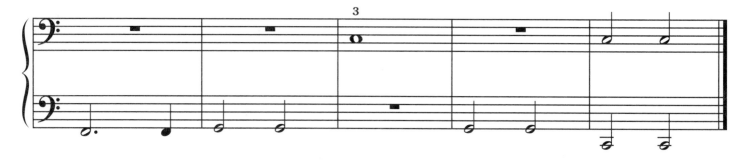

Part 1

Part 2